High Technology
Wearable Technology

by Julie Murray

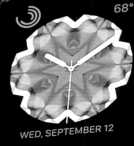

68°

WED, SEPTEMBER 12

11AM 5K TRAINING

10:09

Running Tunes

3

Dash!
LEVELED READERS
An Imprint of Abdo Zoom • abdobooks.com

3 Dash!
LEVELED READERS

Level 1 – Beginning
Short and simple sentences with familiar words or patterns for children who are beginning to understand how letters and sounds go together.

Level 2 – Emerging
Longer words and sentences with more complex language patterns for readers who are practicing common words and letter sounds.

Level 3 – Transitional
More developed language and vocabulary for readers who are becoming more independent.

THIS BOOK CONTAINS RECYCLED MATERIALS

abdobooks.com

Published by Abdo Zoom, a division of ABDO, PO Box 398166, Minneapolis, Minnesota 55439.
Copyright © 2021 by Abdo Consulting Group, Inc. International copyrights reserved in all countries.
No part of this book may be reproduced in any form without written permission from the publisher.
Dash!™ is a trademark and logo of Abdo Zoom.

Printed in the United States of America, North Mankato, Minnesota.
052020
092020

Photo Credits: Alamy, AP Images, Getty Images, Granger Collection, iStock, Shutterstock,
©Isabelle Grosjean p.9 / CC BY-SA 3.0
Production Contributors: Kenny Abdo, Jennie Forsberg, Grace Hansen, John Hansen
Design Contributors: Dorothy Toth, Neil Klinepier, Laura Graphenteen

Library of Congress Control Number: 2019956154

Publisher's Cataloging in Publication Data

Names: Murray, Julie, author.
Title: Wearable technology / by Julie Murray
Description: Minneapolis, Minnesota : Abdo Zoom, 2021 | Series: High technology | Includes online resources and index.
Identifiers: ISBN 9781098221201 (lib. bdg.) | ISBN 9781098222185 (ebook) | ISBN 9781098222673 (Read-to-Me ebook)
Subjects: LCSH: Wearable technology--Juvenile literature. | Wearables (Wearable technology)--Juvenile literature. | Smart materials--Juvenile literature. | High technology--Juvenile literature. | Technological innovations--Juvenile literature.
Classification: DDC 621.381--dc23

Table of Contents

Wearable Technology

What do eye glasses, hearing aids, and smart watches have in common? They are all wearable technology!

A wearable is a device that is worn on the body. The technology in the wearable can do many things. Keeping track of fitness levels and navigating directions are just a few.

7

Eye glasses were the first wearable technology. They were invented in the 1200s. Wristwatches came out in the 1600s. Wearables have greatly **advanced** since then.

How It Works

Today, a wearable has sensors that gather information about the person wearing it. Some sensors track movement. Others keep track of a person's body temperature or blood sugar levels.

HEART RATE

Measuring

120 bpm

11

Some wearables need to be connected to the internet. This allows them to give directions, play music or receive email. Most wearables use wireless technology. **Bluetooth** and WiFi are examples of this.

Application software, or an app, is available for wearables. Apps can collect and store **data**. They can also be used for communication.

Products

A smart watch is one of the most popular wearables. It can be used for many different things. It can keep track of how many steps you have taken and get your text messages.

16:34

MESSAGES

Jane
I'm on my way.

Rep

Dism

Clothes can be wearables too! Some clothes can keep track of your heart rate and your sleep patterns. There are even shoes that will analyze the way you run.

Wearables are also used in the medical field. They can track **seizures** and measure oxygen levels. They can also send alerts if needed.

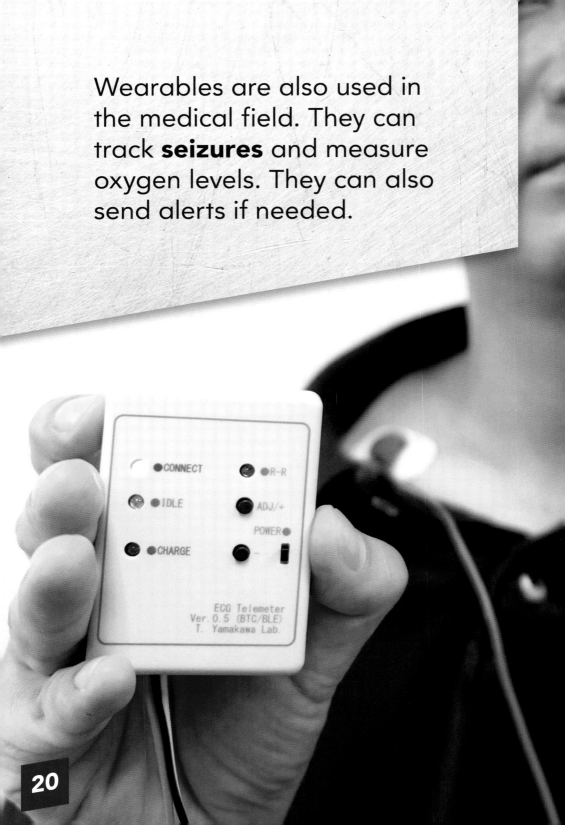

CONNECT
R-R
IDLE
ADJ/+
POWER
CHARGE
–
ECG Telemeter
Ver. 0.5 (BTC/BLE)
T. Yamakawa Lab.

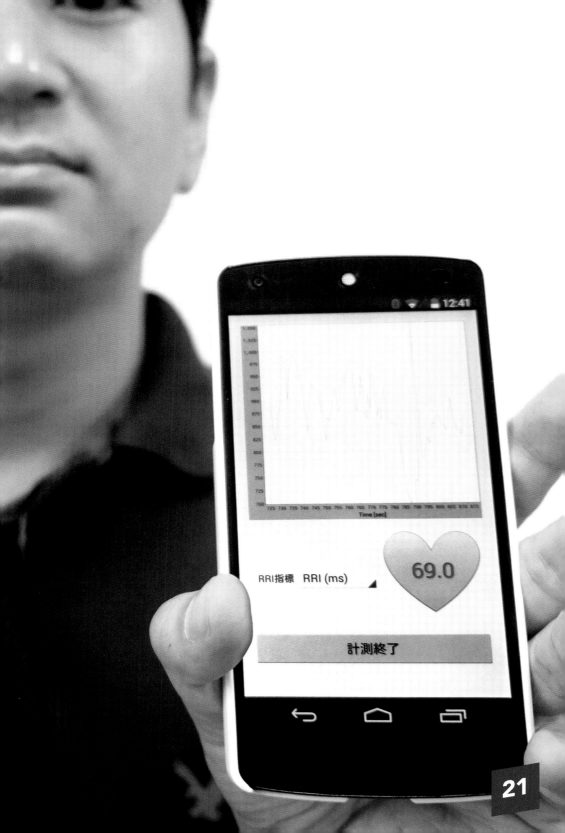

More Facts

- Google Glass acts like a hands-free smartphone. It works through touch and voice commands. It came out in 2013.

- The first **Bluetooth** headset was sold in 2014.

- Impact football helmets are being used today. They can detect hits to the head and warn of concussions.

Glossary

advanced – not in a begging or early state, but in a very developed state.

application software – app for short, software that performs a specific task for a user.

Bluetooth – a short-range radio technology that allows computer, mobile phones, and other devices to communicate with each other.

data – facts, figures, or other pieces of information that can be used to learn something.

seizure – a sudden attack of illness caused by a disorder such as epilepsy.

Index

Online Resources

Booklinks
NONFICTION NETWORK
FREE! ONLINE NONFICTION RESOURCES

To learn more about wearable technology, please visit **abdobooklinks.com** or scan this QR code. These links are routinely monitored and updated to provide the most current information available.